SPORTS GREAT
WILL
CLARK

—Sports Great Books—

SPORTS GREAT WILL CLARK

Ron Knapp

—Sports Great Books—

ENSLOW PUBLISHERS, INC.

Bloy St. & Ramsey Ave. P.O. Box 38

Box 777   Aldershot

Hillside, N.J. 07205 Hants GU12 6BP

U.S.A.   U.K.

Library of Congress Cataloging-in-Publication Data

Knapp, Ron.
    Sports great Will Clark / Ron Knapp.
        p. cm. — (Sports great books)
    Includes index.
    Summary: A biography of one of the best hitters in major league baseball who became
the game's highest-paid player in 1989.
    ISBN 0-89490-390-X
    1. Clark, Will, 1964– —Juvenile literature. 2. Baseball players—United States—
Biography—Juvenile literature. [1. Clark, Will, 1964– . 2. Baseball players.] I. Title. II.
Series.
GV865.C438K58 1993
796.357'092—dc20

                                                                                92-521
                                                                                  CIP
                                                                                   AC
Printed in the United States of America

10 9 8 7 6 5 4 3 2 1

Photo Credits: Ron Knapp, p. 53; Mitchell Layton Photography, pp. 24, 28, 38, 43, 55, 56,
58; Mississippi State University, pp. 17, 19, 20; Oakland Athletics, pp. 21, 45, 46; Saint
Louis Cardinals, pp. 27, 36; San Francisco Giants, pp. 8, 9, 10, 12, 32, 34, 48.

Cover Photo: Mitchell Layton Photography

Contents

Chapter 1

It was the kind of game for which Will Clark lived. His team, the San Francisco Giants, were battling the Cubs at Chicago's Wrigley Field in the first game of the 1989 National League Championship Series.

"I thrive on pressure situations," Clark said. "Usually with men on base." San Francisco led 4–3 in the fourth inning. Clark watched anxiously from the dugout. The Giants had runners at second and third with just one out. A hit would break the game open and give his team a big lead. Will had to wait his turn to bat because two teammates would come up before him. "I love those situations," he said. "I can't wait to get up there when there are men on base."

Chicago manager Don Zimmer signaled to his pitcher Greg Maddux that he wanted him to walk Brett Butler. A walk would load the bases and make it much easier to turn a groundout into a double play, which would end the inning without letting the Giants score. Butler went to first, and Robby Thompson stepped to the plate. Clark picked up his bat and headed for the on-deck circle. If Thompson didn't hit into

Will enjoys batting with runners on base.

a double play. Maddux would have to pitch to Clark, who was having a great night at the plate. He'd already doubled in a run in the first inning and hit a solo homer in the third.

Thompson was out on a short pop fly, and the runners held. Clark would get his wish. He was going to bat with the two outs and the bases loaded. Zimmer called time so he could walk to the mound and tell Maddux what to throw. The Cub manager didn't realize that Clark was standing near home plate watching them. He could read Maddux's lips so he knew Maddux was going to throw an inside fastball. When the pitch came, Clark was ready. He slammed the ball into the street behind the right field bleachers. By the time he crossed home plate behind three of his teammates, the score was 8–3. Roger Craig, the Giant manager, greeted Clark in front of the dugout with the rest of the team. It wasn't the first time he had seen his first baseman get a big hit. Craig knew Will was one of the most intense competitors in baseball.

Giant manager Roger Craig says
Will Clark is a great competitor.

Kevin Mitchell and Will figured Mitch Williams would be throwing fastballs in the 1989 National League Championship Series.

When the game was over, Clark had four hits and six runs batted in (RBIs), a play-off record. One sportswriter called Clark "a one-man wrecking crew."

Unfortunately for the Cubs, Clark wasn't finished with them yet. Five days later, the Giants led the Championship Series three games to one. All they needed was one more win. The game was tied 1–1 in the bottom of the eighth inning. Once again the bases were loaded, and Clark was the batter. More than 62,000 Giant fans shook Candlestick Park with their cheers.

Zimmer sent in ace reliever Mitch "Wild Thing" Williams. Clark and Kevin Mitchell, the next batter, watched the new pitcher warm up. They knew Williams was a fastball pitcher and that was the pitch they expected him to use.

"It was the Wild Thing vs. Will the Thrill," reported *Sports Illustrated.* "Baseball doesn't get any better than this."

After two quick strikes and a ball the Wild Thing threw a high fastball, which Clark fouled back. Another high fastball and another foul. Clark was waiting for the pitch he wanted to hit.

Vin Scully, the television announcer, said, "In every important series there's a moment where it becomes difficult to breathe and swallow. This is that moment."

Clark stepped back from the plate and took a deep breath. When he stepped back into the batter's box Williams threw another fastball. This time Clark slammed it right back up the middle. Two runs scored and the Giants led 3–1.

"We've all seen supreme athletes in all sports rise to the occasion," Craig said after the game. "But you won't see what he did today." In one of the biggest games of the year, Clark had been down two strikes against one of the best left-handed pitchers in baseball. Once again he had come through with the big hit.

Will batted .650 in the 1989 championship series.

In the top of the ninth, the Cubs got two outs before Curtis Wilkerson singled. The Giants needed just one more out, but Mitch Webster came through with a single, and the Cubs had runners on first and third. Jerome Walton singled, Wilkerson scored, and the Giant lead was down to one run, 3–2. The tying run was on second base, and the next batter was Ryne Sandberg, a .290 hitter and the Cubs' most valuable player. Clark was afraid the game was slipping away. He walked to the mound and shouted to Steve Bedrosian, the relief pitcher. "It's your game! And you're going to win it!"

Bedrosian must have been convinced. Soon Sandberg was out, the Championship Series was over, and the Giants had their first pennant in twenty-seven years.

During the five games with Chicago. Clark went 13-for-20 for a .650 batting average. He had two home runs and eight RBIs. He was named the Championship Series Most Valuable Player. Clark didn't really want to talk about his fine performance. "Winning it all is what really mattered," he said.

With the Championship Series behind them, what really mattered to all the Giants was beating the Oakland Athletics, champions of the American League, in the World Series. They called it the "Battle of the Bay" since the two teams are neighbors. Oakland is just east of San Francisco Bay, on the Pacific coast.

The World Series would prove to be a disappointment for the San Francisco Giants. After it had been interrupted by a disastrous earthquake, the outcome didn't seem all that important, anyway. Clark was upset when the Giants didn't beat the Athletics, but he expected to play in many more World Series games. After all, he was only twenty-five and he'd been a major league player for only four years. He was confident the Giants had the talent to make it back to the World Series.

13

Chapter 2

William Nuschler Clark, Jr., was born in New Orleans, Louisiana, on March 13, 1964. To avoid confusion with his father, Bill, he was nicknamed Will.

Young Will learned to hunt and fish from his dad. They spent almost every weekend in the woods or near the water. That didn't leave much time for baseball, but Will didn't mind. He never even thought about playing major league baseball until he was a junior in high school.

Will was a good hunter because his eyesight was so sharp. His father said he shot ducks before anybody else could even see them. After becoming a star for the San Francisco Giants, Will said he believed all those years of following birds in the sights of his rifle helped prepare him for following the flight of a baseball from a pitcher's hand to the plate.

Besides hunting and fishing, Bill Clark also taught his son to be a competitor. When he was younger, Bill was a fine athlete who separated his shoulder playing football. After that, he stuck to pool, a game that was a lot less dangerous. But Bill didn't play pool just for fun. He played to win, and his son was the same way. When Will joined the San Francisco Giants, he got a reputation as one of the most intense competitors in baseball. When he was on the field, nothing mattered except doing everything he could to win the game. He did his best when the pressure was on. The Clarks say he got that attitude from his father.

The Clarks claimed that Will became a first baseman because of Flash, the family's black Labrador retriever. When Will was only four years old, Flash came home carrying a left-handed first baseman's mitt in his mouth. Bill and his wife Letty were embarrassed. They didn't want their dog stealing things from the neighbors. They tried to find out where the mitt had come from, but nobody in the neighborhood had ever seen it before. They ran an ad in the local newspaper describing the mitt, but nobody called. Finally, since Will was a left-hander, they gave the mitt to him.

A few weeks later, Flash brought home another left-handed first baseman's mitt, but this one was brand new. The Clarks tried once again to discover where Flash had found the mitt, but once again they had no luck. Flash never brought home anything else, but that was all the baseball equipment Will needed. When his hand was big enough, he began to use the gloves. Since he had a first baseman's mitt, that was the spot he took in the field.

The Clark family had moved around before finally settling back in New Orleans. The children got used to making new friends. Later Will went to a different high school than the rest of his elementary classmates. When he went to college he was the only person from his high school to choose Mississippi State University. Will believes attending the different schools and meeting lots of people helped make him self-confident. He was never shy or quiet.

Will grew up in Louisiana, hunting and fishing with his dad and playing baseball with the mitts Flash brought him. During the summers, he played on local teams that made it to the Babe Ruth World Series and the American Legion World Series. He attended Jesuit High School in New Orleans, where he was a star on the baseball team. In 1982, when he was a senior, he had ten home runs and 32 RBIs. That was good enough to earn him honors as a High School All-American.

The Kansas City Royals thought he was good enough to someday play major league baseball. They selected him in the fourth round of the amateur draft. That meant they were the only team that could sign him to a contract, but Will decided he wasn't ready to be a professional. He gave up a chance to play as a professional so that he could attend Mississippi State University and play college baseball.

In 1984, only his second year at college, Will was an All-American for the Bulldogs. He hit 28 home runs and had

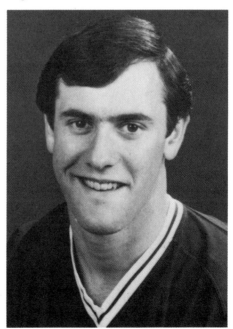

Will gave up the chance to sign a contract with the Kansas City Royals so that he could play baseball at Mississippi State University.

93 RBIs and a .368 batting average. That spring he and 4,000 other players tried out for a spot on the United States Olympic team. Will was one of the twenty players to make it.

The Olympic team had a pair of first basemen, Clark and Mark McGwire, who had hit 31 homers for the University of Southern California. Rod Dedeaux, the Olympic coach, decided he wanted both players in the lineup for every game. They usually took turns playing first base and being the designated hitter. Sometimes Dedeaux moved them all over the field. Clark enjoyed the chance to play other positions. "They've used me everywhere," he said. He played right field, left field, and first base.

Before the Olympic Games began, the team played thirty-two games across the country against college, amateur, and minor league teams. Will's best game was at Fenway Park, the home of the Boston Red Sox, where he hit three homers. He hoped that someday he'd have a chance to be a pro player in a place like Fenway Park. "I could make a living hitting here."

He probably enjoyed a game back in Jackson, Mississippi the most. Most of the 5,800 fans in the stadium were there to cheer for their hometown hero. Bill and Letty Clark had come to the game, too. When Will was introduced, the hometown crowd game him a standing ovation.

Will tipped his cap and flashed a wide grin. "It was nice to be home," he said. "I told myself . . . if this couldn't get me pumped up, then nothing would." Early in the game, he beat out an infield single and then doubled. In the sixth inning, with the Olympic team ahead 8–2, Clark slapped another hit through the infield. Instead of playing it safe with a single, he never stopped at first. He wanted another double. The throw came in at second, and he looked out, but he beat the tag by diving head first into the bag. The crowd stood and cheered again. After the game, he was asked why he had bothered to stretch the hit into a double when his team was already ahead by six runs. Clark thought it was a stupid question. "I don't walk out there and not give 110 percent," he said.

Fans across the nation cheered Will and the rest of the Olympic team. The only town he didn't like was San Francisco. "Those were the worst fans I've ever seen," he said. They booed Will and his teammates when they made errors and didn't get hits. "I thought that was kind of bush." Of course, Clark didn't know that one day he would be a superstar for the San Francisco Giants and one of the most popular athletes in the city.

Will and Rafael Palmeiro were teammates on the 1985 Mississippi State Bulldogs.

The USA team won 27 of 32 games in the pre-Olympic tour. Clark led the team with a .392 average, 13 home runs, and 35 RBIs. McGwire, the other first baseman and the man who would one day play pro ball for the Oakland Athletics, batted .391.

In Olympic competition at Dodger Stadium in Los Angeles, the American team won its first three games against Taiwan, Italy, and the Dominican Republic by a combined score of 30–2. Then Clark singled, stole second, and scored as the USA beat Korea 5–2. Things didn't go so well in the final game for the gold medal, however. Will failed to get a hit in

Will, Bobby Thigpen, and Jeff Brantley were former Mississippi State players chosen to participate in the 1990 All-Star Game.

Mark McGwire was Will's teammate on the 1984 Olympic squad. He later played for the Oakland Athletics.

four at bats, and Japan won 6–3. The American team had to be satisfied with second place and the silver medal.

In the fall of 1984, Clark returned to Mississippi State for his junior year. That spring he had a .420 average, 25 home runs, and 77 RBIs. As soon as the season was over, he was drafted again, this time by the San Francisco Giants. This time he decided he was ready to play big league ball.

Chapter 3

Will Clark was a very talented twenty-year-old, but the San Francisco Giants decided he needed to spend time on a minor league team before playing big league ball. They assigned him to their Class A team in Fresno, California.

On June 21, 1985, Clark joined the team for a game against Visalia. When he walked to the plate for the first time, he wanted to prove he didn't belong in the minors for long. He blasted the first pitch for a home run. Before the game was over, he hit another. By the end of the season, he had 10 homers, had knocked in 48 runs, and batted .309. Fresno won the California League title.

As soon as the Class A season was over, the Giants sent him to the Arizona Instructional League, where he could get extra practice during the winter. He played only 10 games, but he had 3 home runs, 19 RBIs, and a .487 batting average. After that, the Giants decided they had seen enough. They sent him home to rest. They wanted him to be ready for the 1986 National League season. Even though he had played only 65

Giants' coach Roger Craig was confident enough in Clark to take a chance on starting him at first base.

minor league games, Clark was moving up to the major leagues in San Francisco.

When spring training started, Will told the other players that not only would he make the team, but he was also going to be San Francisco's starting first baseman. After impressing Manager Roger Craig, he earned the job. Some people wondered if he was ready, but as usual Will himself was confident.

Clark was good, but he was also lucky. The Giants had lost 100 games in 1985, and Craig was willing to take risks with new players. If San Francisco had been a winning team, there probably wouldn't have been room for rookie players.

Clark wanted to prove that he deserved to be the starting first baseman. On April 8, 1986, the Giants opened against Nolan Ryan and the Houston Astros at the Astrodome. In his first at bat, Will looked at a ball and a strike and then, in his first swing as a major leaguer, knocked a Ryan fastball into the seats for a home run. After the game, he told reporters how much he had enjoyed his first game. When they couldn't think of anything else to ask him, he said, "Don't you have any more questions? I've got more answers." A week later, in his first game at Candlestick Park in San Francisco, he homered again.

By then he was getting a lot of attention from the fans and the press. Nobody doubted that he had plenty of confidence in his abilities or that he wanted to do his best every time he came up to the plate. "Sometimes he gets a base hit and is upset because he was doing something wrong," said teammate Mike Krukow.

When he wasn't playing or practicing baseball, Will tried to keep his hunting skills sharp by shooting skeet in San Francisco. A machine propelled 100 clay pigeons into the air, one at a time. Clark could usually hit 97 or 98 out of 100. The only thing he didn't like about playing for San Francisco was that it kept him away from Louisiana where he loved to hunt and fish.

The rookie from New Orleans was popular in San Francisco. When his batting average stayed around .300, he was recognized around the league as a star. Chris Berman, an announcer on ESPN, nicknamed him "The Natural" after the mythical star Roy Hobbes in the movie starring Robert Redford. Teammate Bob Brenley gave him the name "Will the Thrill." Clark liked that. He put THRILL on the back of his helmet. When he wasn't at his apartment, friends who called got his answering machine and heard the old song "The Thrill Is Gone."

Manager Craig was glad he had put the Thrill into the starting lineup. "He has one of the prettiest swings you'll ever see," he said. "He reminds me of Stan Musial." Musial was a great outfielder who had a career batting average of .331 with the St. Louis Cardinals. Craig believed Will had the talent to someday lead the league in hitting or home runs.

Some of the other Giant players, however, resented all the attention Clark was getting. They made fun of the cowboy boots he loved to wear. Once while he was practicing, some of them spray-painted the boots orange. Will tried to be a good sport about the teasing. He just laughed when he discovered the boots, and soon the players replaced them. His teammates made fun of his high-pitched voice by nicknaming him "Will the Shrill." Clark laughed at that, too. "I don't mind the flak at all, the pranks," he said. "I think it keeps everybody loose."

Clark tried to get along with all his teammates, but he never liked Jeffrey Leonard, the big leftfielder. "He was on me so much," Clark said. On June 3, he suffered his first serious injury when he collided with first baseman Andres Galarraga of the Montreal Expos. The doctors told him he had

Will was compared to Stan Musial, the Hall of Famer who played with the St. Louis Cardinals.

In his first time at bat in the major leagues, Clark amazingly homered off superstar pitcher Nolan Ryan. Clark began his career with a bang.

a hyperextended left elbow, and the Giants put him on the disabled list. He missed forty-seven games while the elbow healed. While Clark was sitting out, Leonard told him he wouldn't be needing his bats for a while so he threw them into a trash can.

Will returned to action in the middle of July, but his elbow still bothered him. It was difficult for him to hit the ball solidly. He finished his first season in the majors with 11 home runs, 41 RBIs, and a .287 batting average. His performance helped the Giants win 83 games, 21 more than they'd won the year before. Instead of finishing last in the National League West, San Francisco was third.

As soon as the season ended, Will had surgery on his elbow to remove bone and cartilage fragments remaining from his collision with Galarraga. Back home in New Orleans, he worked out during the winter with a conditioning expert. By spring training, the elbow was as good as new, and he was ready for the 1987 season.

Chapter 4

If it hadn't been for his feud with Jeffrey Leonard and the way the season ended, 1987 would have been almost a perfect year for Will Clark. He blasted 35 home runs and batted .308 as the San Francisco Giants won the National League West.

Clark and Leonard had never gotten along, but late in the season, they got into a fistfight in the Giants' clubhouse. Their teammates had to pull them apart, but neither of them was injured. Clark said it was no big deal, just two athletes who didn't like each other. He wanted to forget the whole incident. Leonard, who is black, was still angry two years later. He said Clark was prejudiced.

Clark also had a heated argument with another black teammate, Chris Brown. They didn't swing at each other, but Clark called him a racial name. Manager Roger Craig said Will lost his temper and said some things he didn't really mean. Clark realized he had been wrong. He apologized to Brown and the entire Giants team.

Clark admitted he sometimes used words he shouldn't, but he denied being prejudiced. He said race wasn't important to

Manager Roger Craig sometimes wasn't pleased with Clark's behavior.

him and that he had many black friends. Kevin Mitchell, another black teammate, defended his friend Will. He said he and Clark were like brothers.

Will always had a lot to say when he was on the field, too. When he made an out, he sometimes lost his temper. He yelled at his teammates, the fans, the umpires, and the reporters. Mitchell and most of the other Giants were glad to have him around. They said his yelling helped motivate them to play their best.

After making an out, Clark would sometimes yell swear words at himself on the way back to the dugout. Some fans complained because they didn't want their children in the stadium to hear that kind of talk. The Giants asked him to clean up his language when he was near the stands. Craig wasn't always happy with his first baseman's behavior. "He's got some growing up to do," he said. He had many discussions with Clark about controlling his temper. Will knew Craig was right, and he tried to behave himself. He began keeping his mouth shut when he was next to the stands, but he kept yelling on the field and in the dugout.

Clark also tried to become a smarter player by learning from other players. He liked to watch good hitters like Wade Boggs and Tony Gwynn. He also spent a lot of time with San Francisco's two main pinch hitters, Joel Youngblood and Harry Spillman. They'd had a lot of experience batting in pressure situations. He liked to talk to Mike Krukow about pitching strategy. He wanted to know what pitches to expect in different situations.

Craig said Clark's efforts were bearing fruit. He became much more patient at the plate. He tried not to swing at the first pitch unless it was right over the plate. It became harder for pitchers to fool him with a pitch he didn't expect.

Kevin Mitchell said Will treated him like a brother.

Clark himself said one of his problems was his position in the batting order. Craig liked to change his lineup almost everyday to keep his opponents guessing. Sometimes Will batted in the lead-off position, and sometimes he batted seventh. He wished he had the same spot every day.

In 1987, Clark was one of the big reasons San Francisco made it to the National League Championship Series with the St. Louis Cardinals. He was at his best the first week in August when he got five homers and ten RBIs to earn "National League Player of the Week" honors.

Then in the first game of the Championship Series, the Cardinals scored three runs in the sixth inning to give them a 5–2 lead. Two innings later, the Giants threatened when Robby Thompson walked and Leonard singled. Candy Maldonado's double scored Thompson to make it 5–3. Chilli Davis walked, and the bases were loaded for Clark. A single could tie the game. It was the kind of pressure situation Clark loved, but his time he didn't come through. He flew out to right field, and the inning was over. Craig was surprised when there was no more scoring and the Giants lost. "I don't think they're a better ball club than we are. But they're one up."

In the second game, Clark's second-inning home run gave San Francisco a 2–0 lead. Leonard also homered, but was loudly booed by the St. Louis fans for comments he had made about the Cardinals. They also hated the way he ran the bases after his homer. They thought he was showing off by running slowly with one arm held tightly at his side. Leonard said the booing didn't bother him. "I love it," he said. "It pumps me up."

Leonard and Maldonado opened the eighth inning with singles. After Eddie Miller's sacrifice bunt, there were runners on second and third. Clark was up, but the Cardinals walked him intentionally. The bases were still loaded after Bob

Ozzie Smith's error helped the Giants beat the Cardinals in the second game of the 1987 National League Championship Series.

Melvin struck out. Jose Uribe grounded the ball to St. Louis shortstop Ozzie Smith. The ball rolled through his legs, allowing Leonard and Maldonado to score. The Giants won 5–0.

Leonard's third homer of the series helped give San Francisco a 4–0 lead early in Game 3. Jim Linderman's home run cut the lead to 4–2 in the sixth. Five straight Cardinal singles put the Cards ahead 6–4 an inning later. The Giants got a solo homer in the ninth from Harry Spillman, but lost 6–5.

Before the fourth game, Craig had a talk with his team. "I just told them that our backs were against the wall, and that's when we played our best ball this year." For the fourth straight game, Leonard homered, and the Giants won 4–2 to even the series at two games apiece. Krukow, the winning pitcher, thought San Francisco was going to win it all. "The pressure is on . . . " he said. "But it sure is fun."

The Cardinals led the fifth game 3–2 until Joe Price shut them out for the last five innings. Uribe's two-run single helped the Giants storm back to take a 6–3 victory. Clark singled, giving him a hit in each of the first five play-off games. San Francisco was one game away from earning a spot in the World Series.

When the Championship Series moved back to Busch Stadium, Clark said he enjoyed the cool October air in St. Louis. "I like this weather." But Clark didn't get a hit in Game 6 and the Giants lost 1–0. The Cardinal fans tried to upset Leonard by throwing beer, coins, hot dogs, and even cowbells at him as he stood in the outfield. "They could throw the whole bleachers at me." Leonard said. "I'm not coming out of this game. I want to win." The Cardinals were embarrassed by their fans. John Tudor said he thought Leonard was a jerk, but nobody deserved the treatment he was getting in St. Louis.

The 1987 Championship Series was a disappointment for Will and the rest of the Giants.

The deciding game of the Championship Series was a nightmare for the Giants. For the second straight game, they failed to score a run, and St. Louis won 6–0. The Cardinals and not the Giants had earned a trip to the World Series against the Minnesota Twins. "I never would have believed it," said Craig.

Leonard was named the series Most Valuable Player, but he was very disappointed. He said something that even Will Clark would have agreed with. "There's not a Giants player in here who won't have a long, long winter."

Chapter 5

Will Clark and the San Francisco Giants hoped 1988 would be the year they made it to the World Series. Once again Clark had a fine year. In May, he hit homers in three straight games. On June 22, he knocked in seven runs in a single game against the San Diego Padres. When he came to bat in the ninth, the bases were loaded, and the Giants trailed by two. He slammed a double that emptied the bases and won the game 8–7.

Clark was elected to play in his first All-Star game. When the season was over, he had 109 RBIs, tops in the National League. He also had 29 homers and a .282 batting average. The Giants voted him the most valuable player on the team. Despite his fine statistics, San Francisco finished fourth in the Western Division with an 83–79 record.

In 1989, Clark was hot right from the start. He had five hits, including a double and a homer, as he drove in three runs on April 23 in Los Angeles. After he batted .351 with six home runs and 24 RBIs in May, he was chosen National League Player of the Month. He received more votes than any other National League player as he was elected to play in his second straight All-Star Game.

On September 21, he collided with Los Angeles' Mike Scioscia at home plate and limped off the field with a bruised knee. For three games, he sat on the bench to give the knee time to heal. It was the first time he had missed a game in almost two years.

By the time he was back in the lineup, sports fans all over the country had noticed the battle he was having with San Diego's Tony Gwynn for the National League batting championship. After getting the league's highest average in 1984, 1987, and 1988, Gwynn was already recognized as one of the top hitters in the game. He wanted another batting title in 1989, but he knew it was going to be tough to beat Clark. "Will's a great hitter who's never won the batting title," Gwynn said, "but I think he really wants it."

Before the season even began, Clark had decided to raise his average by trying to hit the ball to all fields instead of always pulling it to right field. "It's changed me a ton," he said. "It's made me a more complete hitter." His strategy worked. By the middle of September, the last full month of the season, he and Gwynn were both hitting around .340.

Clark worked on his batting even when he wasn't on the field. After each game, he made notes on the pitches he received and the hits and outs he had made each time he batted. He also studied videotapes of pitchers facing him. He knew it would not be easy to beat Gwynn. "Right now, he has the tightest swing in the National League," Clark said.

The race between Clark and Gwynn went down to the wire. The Giants were in San Diego the final weekend of the season, so the two players could keep a close eye on each other. In the last two games, Clark got two hits, but Gwynn got six, and the Padre star won his fourth batting title, .336 to

Clark worked hard to raise his batting average. He and Tony Gwynn battled for the highest batting average title of 1989.

.333. Clark was disappointed but didn't have a problem losing to a competitor like Gwynn. "Tony Gwynn beat me," he said. "He got six hits the last two days, and he beat me clean."

San Francisco won the Western Division and then destroyed the Chicago Cubs four games to one in the National League Championship Series. Clark, of course, was the series MVP. He set records with his .650 batting average, 13 hits, and 8 runs scored. Cubs' manager Don Zimmer said, "Will Clark did some damage, a lot of damage, but that's not unusual for him."

Clark and the rest of the Giants looked forward to facing the Oakland Athletics in the "Battle of the Bay" World Series. A few days before the first game, Clark's mouth got him into trouble again. In an interview with reporters, he insulted his former teammate Jeffrey Leonard who was now with the Seattle Mariners. "We got rid of him," Clark said. "Now look where we are." Fans remembered that the two of them had never gotten along, but nobody understood why Clark was trying to keep the feud alive.

After that, Clark decided not to say anything more about Leonard. In fact, he didn't say much more about anything. He had tonsillitis and it hurt too much to talk.

Clark was quiet in the World Series opener, but so were the Giants' bats. San Francisco didn't even get a runner as far as third base until the last inning. Oakland scored in the second when Dave Henderson walked, followed by singles from Terry Steinbach and Tony Phillips. Walt Weiss hit a slow grounder to Clark, who made a bad throw to the plate, forcing catcher Terry Kennedy out of position. Steinbach slid into Kennedy's mitt, knocking the ball loose for the second Oakland run. Rickey Henderson's single made it 3–0. Dave Stewart shut the Giants out, and the Athletics finally won 5–0. Clark croaked, "We ran into a buzz saw."

Rickey Henderson— part of Oakland's powerful 1989 squad.

Dave Stewart pitched Oakland to a 5–0 victory over San Francisco in the opening
game of the 1989 World Series.

The second game was more of the same. In the third inning, the score was tied 1–1. The Giants had Brett Butler on third and Clark at the plate. A hit would've put San Francisco ahead for the first time in the series, but Clark struck out. The Giants never got another run, and Oakland won 5–1.

San Francisco fans hoped the Giants' luck would change when the series moved home to Candlestick Park. On October 17, more than 60,000 of them were in the stands ready to cheer their heroes to victory. Millions of people across the United States were watching the pregame show on television as the players warmed up on the field. Suddenly the ground shook and Candlestick Park began to wobble. It was an earthquake.

The first thing to go was the electricity. That meant the TV screens went blank across the country. Fans at home wondered what was happening. A bridge near the stadium collapsed, burying dozens of cars. Buildings fell. Gas mains bent, burst, and exploded. There were fires throughout the Bay area. The players and fans at Candlestick were lucky. When the shaking stopped, the park still stood. But with no electricity, there were no lights, loudspeakers, or scoreboards. There was no way the game could be played.

It was one of the most powerful earthquakes in American history. More than sixty people died, and there was $10 billion worth of property damage. The World Series wasn't resumed for ten days. By then, electricity had been restored to Candlestick Park, and some of the damaged buildings had been cleared away. Clark's tonsillitis had cleared up, but once the third game started, it was obvious there was something wrong with the Giants. San Francisco fell behind 13–3 going into the last inning. Four Giant runs in the ninth made it 13–7, but the Athletics had their third win in a row.

Despite the Giants' loss to the Athletics in the World Series, Will continued to work hard to improve his game.

It took only one more game. Oakland jumped to an 8–0 lead and held on to win 9–6. Terry Kennedy said, "The A's were a tidal wave, and we just couldn't get out of the way." After his spectacular series against the Cubs, Clark's performance in the World Series was disappointing. In four games, he got three singles and one double. No home runs. No RBIs.

Clark and the Giants had a great year in 1989, but they hadn't reached their goal of a World Series title. He took satisfaction from the way his game was improving, year by year. He said he was going to continue to work hard and to become a better player every season.

Chapter 6

A few weeks after the end of the 1989 World Series, Will Clark signed a contract that made him the highest-paid player in the history of baseball. The San Francisco Giants agreed to pay him $15 million to play for four more years.

Some people wondered if any player was worth that kind of money. Al Rosen, the Giants' general manager, wasn't worried. He said the big contract was a bargain for the San Francisco Giants. Rosen had watched Clark play, looked at his statistics, and decided he wanted to keep the young first baseman on his team. In his first four years with San Francisco, Clark had batted .304 and hit 98 home runs. Rosen also knew that Clark was at his best when the pressure was on. Hitting against left-handed pitchers, he batted .450 when there were runners at second and third.

By the time he signed the contract, Clark was already back at home in New Orleans. His months away from baseball were a time to relax and enjoy himself. Away from the fans and reporters, he spent most of his time on a bayou hunting and fishing. He rented three square miles of marsh land and water about an hour's drive from New Orleans. He lived there on his thirty-five-foot-long houseboat.

Duck season in Louisiana lasts from the middle of November until the first week of January. Everyday Clark got up at 5 a.m. and climbed into a canoe with Psycho, his black Labrador retriever. He paddled to one of his duck blinds and, after placing 40 decoys in the water, sat back and waited for dawn.

Inside the blind, Will and Psycho were almost invisible to the ducks flying by. The decoy ducks in the water fooled the real ducks, making them feel safe and bringing them close. Will shot three ducks each morning and then watched Psycho retrieve them. By 7:30 a.m., he was paddling the canoe back to the houseboat.

After lunch, Will fished for speckled trout. Then when it was time for dinner, he cooked the three ducks with onions, pepper, wine, and rice. After that, he had to get to bed early so he'd be ready to wake up early the next morning for more hunting. That's the way his vacation went. The only change to the routine came when he was joined on the houseboat by his thirteen-year-old brother Scotty.

The hunting and fishing must have been good for Clark. When the 1990 season began, he was playing great baseball once again. In the Giants' first three games at Atlanta, he went 7 for 12 and knocked in 5 of the team's runs. On April 21 against San Diego's Bruce Hurst, he got his second homer of the season and the 100th of his career as the Giants won 6–4. But San Francisco didn't win many more in April. By the end of the month, the Giants were 8–12, already 7 games behind the division-leading Cincinnati Reds.

San Francisco whipped the Braves 23–8 on June 8 as Will belted two home runs, but the team never got higher than three and a half games behind the Reds. Clark, however, was the

The bayous of Louisiana are a sportsman's paradise. In places like this, Will Clark relaxes in the off season.

second highest vote getter on the National League All-Star team. For the third straight year, he was the starting first baseman, and for the first time he got a hit, a lead-off single. When the season was over, he'd batted .295 and hit 19 home runs. Once again he'd saved his best for when it counted. With a runner on third and two outs, he batted .500.

After the Giants finished the 1990 season in third place, Clark checked into a hospital for a pair of operations. His tonsils, which had been bothering him for some time, were removed. At the same time doctors repaired a minor nerve problem in his foot. He would have the long winter months ahead to recover in time for the next season.

By the time spring training began in 1991, Clark had five major league seasons behind him. He was still an intense competitor who hated to lose, but he was now twenty-seven, old enough to control his temper and watch what he was saying. He didn't insult opponents and teammates any more. By then, he even found some good things to say about Jeffrey Leonard, the player he had fought in the Giants' clubhouse. He didn't pretend that they had gotten along, but he admitted Leonard was a fine player who always did his best.

On the field, too, he was trying to follow Roger Craig's advice to grow up. Fans sitting by the dugout weren't shocked anymore by the words he yelled at himself after he made an out. In fact, bad language at the ball park now irritated him. On August 20, the Giants were in Houston for a game against the Astros. Once again, even though Clark was having another fine season, they weren't in contention for the pennant. They'd lost three games in a row. The Houston fans booed Clark when he stepped up to the plate. Will didn't mind the booing, but he didn't like some of the things the Astro fans were yelling. "They were cursing and I told them to keep it

The 1991 season saw a new Will Clark. He cleaned up his language on the field and made an effort to control his temper.

Clark's powerful swings have made him a favorite among All-Star voters. In 1991 he won the second-highest number of votes.

clean. Any time you're at a visiting park you expect some of that, but with kids all around I don't like to hear cursing."

As usual, the booing helped fire him up. In the sixth inning, he doubled in a run to tie the game 3–3. Then in the seventh, teammate Dave Anderson singled. Houston's Jimmy Jones loaded the bases with walks to Kevin Bass and Will McGee. Rob Mallicoat relieved Jones to face Clark. Will hit the second pitch into the seats for a grand slam home run. After that, the Houston fans didn't have much more to say. The Giants led 7–3 and would eventually win 9–3. "After I hit the grand slam," Clark said, "they didn't say a word. They just hung their heads."

Once again Clark was an All-Star first baseman, but 1991 was the first season he had ever played on a team with a losing record. The Giants finished fourth with 75–87, 19 games behind the Atlanta Braves. With the team doing poorly, he didn't have as many chances to come to bat in pressure situations. He had to work harder to concentrate on each at bat. He also continued to study videotapes of his batting. He batted .301.

Clark's $15-million contract ran through the end of the 1993 season, but by 1991 he was no longer the highest paid player in baseball. Bobby Bonilla, of the New York Mets, and Ryne Sandberg, of the Chicago Cubs, each had multiyear contracts worth about $30 millon. The Pittsburgh Pirates paid Bobby Bonds $4.7 million for the 1992 season alone. Then in August 1992, Cal Ripken, Jr. of the Baltimore Orioles, agreed to a $30.5 million 5-year contract.

Despite the differences in pay, the Giants and their fans still think Will Clark is among the best players in the game. Rosen is sure Clark is good enough to be compared to other great athletes like Mel Ott, Bill Terry, Willie Mays, Willie

One of the highest-paid players in baseball, Clark is still waiting for a second chance at victory in the World Series.

McCovey, and Juan Marichal who have played for the Giants. He said Will is worth all the millions the team is paying him.

After the 1993 season, Clark will only be 29 years old. He should have many years left in a Giants uniform. By the time his contract is up, Rosen figures he'll deserve a raise. "We'll talk some more," he said, "and then we'll sign another contract, and then he'll be the highest-paid player in baseball again."

CAREER STATISTICS

Year	Team	G	AB	R	H	2B	3B	HR	RBI	SB	AVG.
1985	Fresno *	65	217	41	67	14	0	10	48	11	.309
1986	San Francisco	111	408	66	117	27	2	11	41	4	.287
	Phoenix*	6	20	3	5	0	0	0	1	1	.250
1987	San Francisco	150	529	89	163	29	5	35	91	5	.308
1988	San Francisco	162	575	102	162	31	6	29	109	9	.282
1989	San Francisco	159	588	104	196	38	9	23	111	8	.333
1990	San Francisco	154	600	91	177	25	5	19	95	8	.295
1991	San Francisco	148	565	84	170	32	7	29	116	4	.301
Major League Totals		884	3265	536	985	182	34	146	563	38	.302

*Minor Leagues

Where To Write Will Clark:

Mr. Will Clark
c/o   San Francisco Giants
Candlestick Park
San Francisco, CA 94124

61

Index

Spillman, Harry, 33, 37
Sports Illustrated, 11
Steinbach, Terry, 44
Stewart, Dave, 44

T
Taiwan, 20
Terry, Bill, 57
Thompson, Robby, 7, 9, 35
Tudor, John, 37

U
University of Southern
      California, 18
Uribe, Jose, 37

V
Visalia, California, 23

W
Walton, Jerome, 13
Webster, Mitch, 13
Weiss, Walt, 44
Wilkerson, Curtis, 13
Williams, Mitch, 11
World Series (1987), 39
World Series (1989), 13, 44, 47,
      49
Wrigley Field, 7

Y
Youngblood, Joel, 33

Z
Zimmer, Don, 7, 9, 44